I Miss GRANDMA

Reverend Karen Wright

Archway Publishing books may be ordered through booksellers or by contacting:

Archway Publishing
1663 Liberty Drive
Bloomington, IN 47403
www.archwaypublishing.com
844-669-3957

Because of the dynamic nature of the Internet, any web addresses or links contained in this book may have changed since publication and may no longer be valid. The views expressed in this work are solely those of the author and do not necessarily reflect the views of the publisher, and the publisher hereby disclaims any responsibility for them.

Any people depicted in stock imagery provided by Getty Images are models, and such images are being used for illustrative purposes only.
Certain stock imagery © Getty Images.

ISBN: 978-1-6657-3839-2 (sc)
ISBN: 978-1-6657-3841-5 (hc)
ISBN: 978-1-6657-3840-8 (e)

Print information available on the last page.

Archway Publishing rev. date: 06/12/2023

This book is in memory of "Grandma Jo." JoAnn Bielefeldt Wagner was a loving wife, mother, and grandmother. She loved her family and sought to help others.

Her presence is missed, but her legacy of love for others lives on.

Every time I see a red cardinal, I think about my grandma. Sometimes thinking about her makes me happy, and sometimes it makes me sad. My grandma died, and I miss her.

When we went to see my grandma and grandpa, she would always have toys for me and my twin brother. She would read us books and play with us too. When we visited, Grandma would have pictures of my brother and me that Mommy had sent to her set up on her piano. She had pictures that I had drawn for her there too.

There was a big glass door in the living room at Grandma and Grandpa's house. That was where we would watch the squirrels and birds. Grandma would chase the squirrels away, but she liked to watch the birds. Her favorite was the red cardinal.

One time when we went to see our grandparents, Grandma had a walker. Mommy told us that Grandma had hurt her hip and the walker was to help her get stronger.

5

A few months later, we went for another visit—this time to celebrate our birthdays! We took some of our presents to show Grandma, and she had presents, balloons, and cupcakes for us. Grandma smiled at us. She wanted to see me dance. She watched my brother play with his new golf clubs. But Grandma looked tired.

A few weeks later, Mommy was very sad. She cried a lot. She told me and my brother that Grandma was dying. That meant that Grandma's body was going to stop working.

One night we had a video call with Grandpa and our aunts. They were with Grandma at the hospital. She looked like she was sleeping. Mommy and Momma told us to tell Grandma that we loved her and to tell her goodbye. Mommy said, "Even though Grandma looks like she is sleeping, she can hear you."

Mommy is sad and cries a lot, and Momma is sad too. I am sad, but I try not to cry. I want to be brave. Mommy and Momma tell my brother and me that crying and being sad are OK. They tell us that we all will have lots of feelings and that we need to feel them. There will be times we are sad or sometimes angry. There will be times we will be happy as well. Mommy told me it is good to laugh and play, but it is OK if I am sad too. Sometimes when I am playing, I think about Grandma, and it makes me sad again.

13

14

We went to Grandma and Grandpa's church. There was a worship service to remember Grandma. Sometimes the service is called a funeral or a memorial service. In our church it is called a Witness to the Resurrection. During the service we prayed and sang. The pastor talked about Grandma and how she loved God and showed God's love to others. She also reminded us that God loves us. We said thank you to God for Grandma's life, and we remembered that she was now with God.

During the service, Mommy and Momma cried. So did Grandpa. I think a lot of people cried. I think they all missed my grandma too.

After the service, some of the people there told my brother and me how much Grandma loved us and how she would show them pictures of us. They told us that she would get excited when we were coming to visit.

I asked whether I could draw a picture for Grandma, but I wondered how she would see it. Mommy said we could put it on the piano, where Grandma always put the pictures I made. She said Grandma would know it was from me.

It has been a year since Grandma died. Our family talks about how we miss Grandma and, sometimes I still get sad. Mommy and Momma tell us it is OK to be sad still; sometimes they are sad too. They tell us that the sad feelings will come and go, and that is normal. They remind my brother and me that Grandma loved us and will always love us.

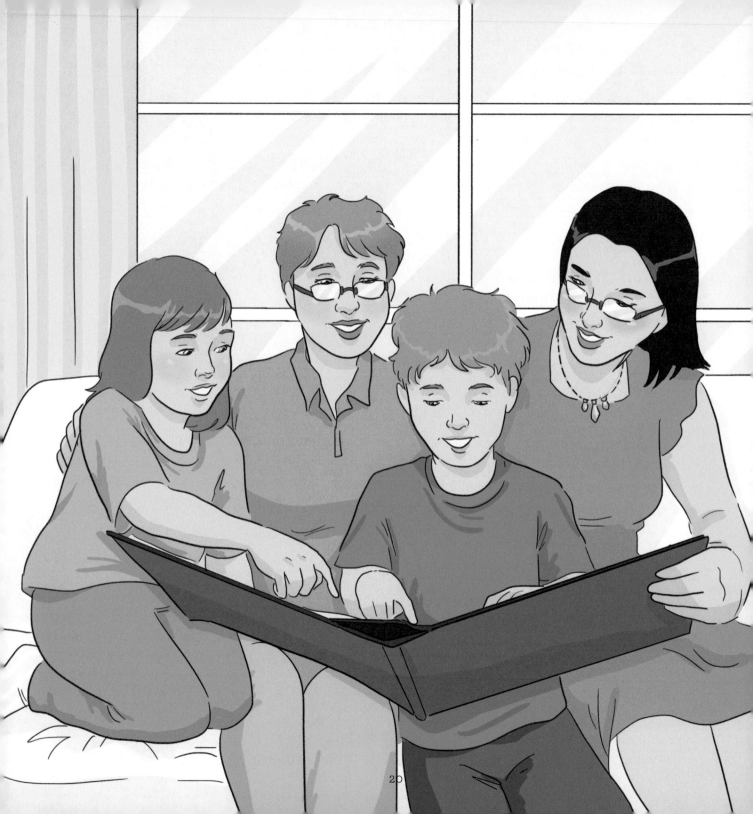

Mommy says when she sees a red cardinal, she thinks about Grandma. Those were Grandma's favorite birds. I look for red cardinals now too. When I see one, I think about Grandma. I think about her smile and her laugh. I remember how much she loves me and my brother. Seeing the cardinal makes me smile, but I still miss Grandma.

For Parents:

This book is written about the death of my mother and the questions that my children asked. Death is never an easy topic to discuss, especially with young children, but it is important. Children grieve differently than adults, and each of us grieves in our own way. It was important to me and my wife (also a pastor) to include the children in our grief process as well. It was important that they saw us feeling sad, angry, happy, or whatever other emotions we experienced. We all shed lots of tears and shared lots of hugs.

Grief is part of a normal process when we experience loss. It comes in waves, sometimes unexpectedly. It is critical that children understand that a roller coaster of emotions is normal and that all the emotions they feel are OK. Drawing or play may be ways in which children can express the feelings they experience.

Printed in the United States
by Baker & Taylor Publisher Services